AF365537

DERYA EDIS / N. MELIS ERAYDIN
HONEY GIRL: RED DRESS

ISBN: 978-605-9218-91-7
1st Edition: June 2021

Original Name: *Bal Kız: Kırmızı Elbise*

TRANSLATION: Şerife Koç
EDITING: Gülnar Mızrak
ILLUSTRATION: N. Melis Eraydın
COVER and PAGE DESIGN: N. Melis Eraydın

GENÇ TUTİ
Bağdat Cad. No:167/2 Çatırlı Apt. B Blok D:4
Göztepe / Kadıköy / İstanbul
Phone: (216) 359 10 20 Fax: (216) 359 40 92
www.tuti.com.tr
tutikitap@tuti.com.tr
 /tutikitap
 /tutikitap
 /tutikitap

Derya Edis
N. Melis Eraydın

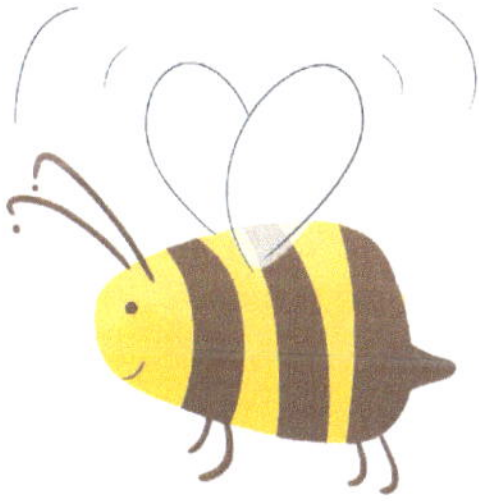

HONEY GIRL
Red Dress

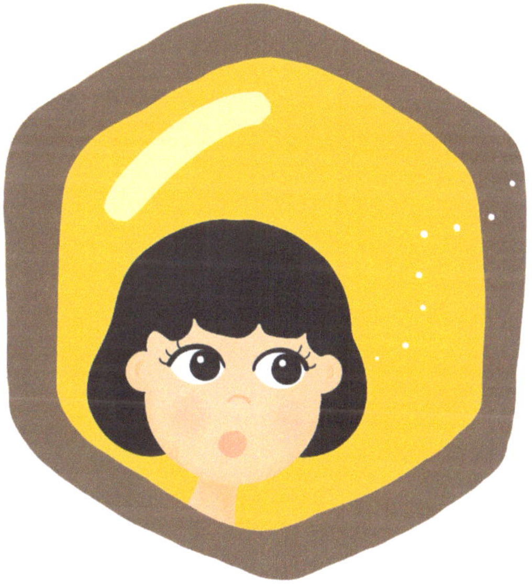

We bees love greeting the rising sun.
First, we fly around our beehive and spread
our wings. Then we look for beautiful flowers
for ourselves for breakfast.

VIZZZZ!

In order to find
the most beautiful flower,
we follow the scents
and fly towards them.

Hmmm!.. The flowers got up early this morning, just like us. Their fragrances are all around.

Mmmmm excellent!

VIZZZ!

Rose scents!

This bee should fly towards that side.

VIZZZ!

Rose scents come from the garden of my grandfather Kenan.

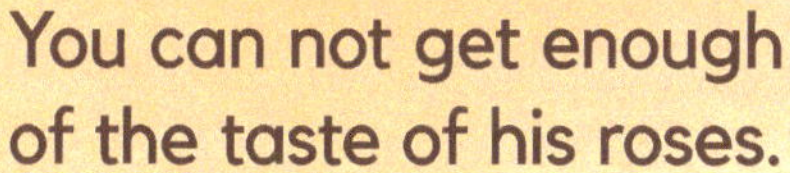

You can not get enough
of the taste of his roses.

· VIZZZZZ! · · ·

My grandfather Kenan
grows such beautiful roses
in this garden that we bees can't
decide which one to start with.

In this beautiful morning,
it's best to have breakfast
with these pink roses.

· VIZZZ! · · ·

Nam Nam Nam! ·

Honey Girl was busy with the game of being a bee, when
she heard her mother's voice:

- My Honey daughter, did you wake up?

- Good morning mummy.

VIZZZ!

- Did my Honey daughter become a bee this morning?

- I became a bee. I flew to the pink roses
of my grandpa Kenan. I had my breakfast.

VIZZZ!

Mother with a smile:

- So you even had breakfast with pink roses. My honey daughter!

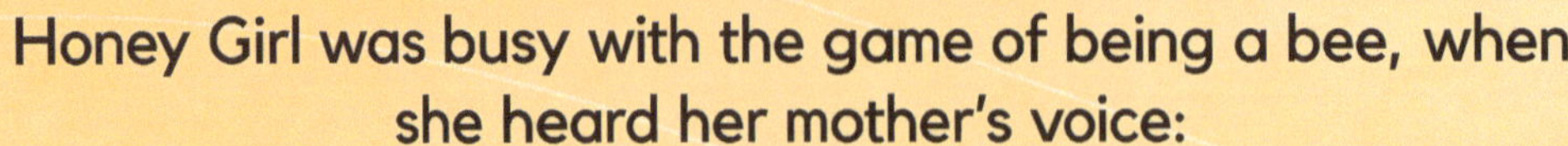

She sat next to Honey Girl on the bed while putting a kiss on her cheek.

- *Was the pollen delicious?*

The Honey Girl buzzed excitedly.

- VIZZZ! *The most delicious.*

The mother opened her hand: *"Don't you have some for me?"* Honey Girl answered excitedly with a smile: *"Don't I !"* Then she pretended to put something in her mother's palm.

While her mother was eating the imaginary pollen in her palm, she was as happy as Honey Girl.

- *Mmmmm! VERY DELICIOUS!*

10

The mother gathered her stuff and stood up
when her imaginary pollen ran out:

*- Come on, my Honey Daughter, first to the bathroom
and then to breakfast. And after you take your medicine,
let's dress you in your new red dress.*

*You have a doctor's appointment today. You don't seem to have
a cough anymore, and moreover you've put on some weight.
You can also walk little by little.*

*This morning is a beautiful morning, my Honey Daughter!
Later, we need to celebrate the occasion.*

Honey Girl was very happy with what she heard.
Because she had had to lie down for a long time. But now
she was healing. Not only has she missed her school and
friends, she also really wanted to put on her red dress and
walk the streets. So,that beautiful morning, she had her
breakfast and took her medicine.

Then came the moment she had been waiting for. Red dress...

Honey Girl loved this dress very much.

While she was sick, her older sister had sewed it up.

She had waited a long time to heal and to wear it.

Her dress was on her when breakfast was over.

She watched herself in admiration before the mirror.

Her mother took the Honey Girl by her hand.
Honey Girl was so happy that her feet hardly touched
the ground as if she was flying.

All the neighbours were happy to see Honey Girl walking
in her red dress. It was as if even the cats, birds, flowers
and trees were happy for her today. Moreover, she was getting
a lot of compliments for her red dress.

They arrived at the doctor's office joyful and happy. The doctor laughed happily when he saw Honey Girl walking in her red dress.

- Ho ho hoooo! Honey Girl! This dress, which takes its color from red rose, looks so good on you! Turn around lightly and let me feast my eyes on you.

Although Honey Girl was a little embarrassed, she turned around
lightly and showed her dress to her doctor.

Her doctor examined Honey Girl.

She was really much better according to what the doctor said.
After months, she has completely healed.

+doctor+

They left the doctor, promising that she would eat healthily,
do sports, and laugh a lot.

On the way home, Honey Girl thought, *"I wish that this day never ends."*
She wanted to share her happiness with all her loved ones.

*- Mommy, will you take me to Nazlı Mum? She will also be very happy
for my geting well, let's have a celebration with Nazlı Mum!*

Nazlı Mum used to live on Honey Girl's street, opposite
the house of Grandpa Kenan. She loved everyone,
especially children, and showed interest and love.
That's why she was the Nazlı Mother of the whole neighborhood.

Honey Girl's mother was very happy with this offer. "*It's a great idea!
Today, instead of flowers let's take you to Nazlı Mum. When she sees
that you are in good health ,she will sit on cloud nine*" she said.

And Honey Girl and her mother were soon at Nazlı Mum's house.

When they entered through the garden door, many children from the neighborhood were eating delicious pastries made by Nazlı Mum in the garden. They all greeted Honey Girl in the Red Dress. They asked enthusiastically:

- Will you play with us now?

Honey Girl happily hugged her friends.

- Yeeess! From now on we'll become bees and fly, we'll become birds and, wing, running we'll cross worlds. I missed you all. What did you do in my absence?

Her friends told Honey Girl how they have saved a cat that had fallen into the loophole. And they said they have learned how to make better kites, how to make paper airplanes.

While they were in deep conversation with each other in the garden, Nazlı Mum of the neighborhood came with another tray of pastry in her hand.

- *Ohhhh! Who has come ! Flowers bloomed in my garden this morning. Honey Girl, you are well healed. Moreover, you walk, run and play.*

Honey Girl ran and hugged Nazlı Mum.

- *I am better Nazlı Mommy.*
We came from the doctor.
He said: Eat healthily, do sports,
and laugh a lot.

Nazlı Mum had Honey Girl sit on her lap,she caressed her with love.
Then she said:

- *Honey Girl, how good this red dress looks on you. Do you know that,
when one becomes very happy and makes others happy, happiness
keeps getting bigger! In the list your doctor gave you, one thing
is missing. While he was saying laugh a lot and smile, he forgot to say
"make also the people around you smile."*

Honey Girl thought to herself that making someone laugh
was also a fun thing. She made both Nazlı Mum and her
friends laugh by making funny faces . They all had a lot of fun.
Nazlı Mum's garden was like a fairground.

After a while Nazlı Mum said:

"How else can we make those around us laugh?"

Everyone thought.

Ali said:

- When I play with my brother, he has a lot of fun and laughs.

Bahar said:

- When I help my mother to set and clear the table, she becomes very happy and always smiles.

Oguz said:

- Sometimes when I give
my younger friends
my shrunken clothes and toys
that I don't play with, they
become very happy and laugh.

Nazlı Mum said:

-When I cook pastry,
the children become very
happy and laugh.

27

Honey Girl thought and thought.
She wondered what she could do to make someone as happy as herself.

While thinking, she couldn't help looking at her friend Zeynep.

Zeynep usually wore old clothes and that day she kept staring at Honey Girl's red dress. At that moment, Honey Girl knew!... She would make Zeynep happy and laugh as much as herself.

She whispered something in her mother's ear and under puzzled glances, they entered Nazlı Mum's house.

When Honey Girl came back , there were other clothes on her.
Her red dress was in her hands. She approached Zeynep.

*- My dear Zeynep, I'm very happy today. I have regained my health,
I wore the red dress today, I have been very happy. Would you be happy
and laugh more if you too wear it?*

Zeynep's beautiful eyes widened with happiness. She hugged Honey Girl,
took the red dress. She immediately ran home and got dressed.

When she returned to the garden, she was bursting with happiness. The red dress looked really good on Zeynep.

• Derya Edis •

The writer who was born in 1975 has worked in various newspapers and magazines as a keeper of archive, a reporter, an editor and an editor-in-chief. Her children's stories, which she has written since 1997, have been published in domestic and foreign children's magazines, especially Red Mouse. She was the guest of the activities of April 23, 2008 in Istanbul Toy Museum with the installation fairy tale exhibition titled "Peace Soup".
In addition, she prepared the "Dream Country" fairy tale project under the social responsibility project for children who could not afford to visit the museum at the Istanbul Toy Museum between September 2009 and November 2012 and taught it. She had the opportunity to reach 2500 children in need with this project every year.

The author, who was entitled to participate in various international competitions, produced works worth exhibiting with "Mirrored Cupboard" and "İdil's Bairam Candy."
The author, who is the editor-in-chief of the Compass Newspaper published in Switzerland, also continues to write and produce for children's publishing as the editor-in-chief of Genç Tuti. Edis, who lives in Indonesia with her family and their dog named Hop, wholeheartedly believes that life itself is a fairy tale. She loves telling tales in her own fairy tale, playing games at every opportunity, laughing and making people laugh... She is trying to grow up with her biggest heroes, her daughters Irmak and Işık...

• Nezahat Melis Eraydın •

She graduated from Mimar Sinan Fine Arts University, Department of Architecture in 2014.
Opening the cover of a children's picture book takes her to the time she misses and places she doesn't know. By making drawings, she wants to be together and take the children she loves the world of them and adults like herself to places they don't know.